Mystic Twine

Mystic Twine

Musings of Mind and Spirit

J. MICHAELS

RESOURCE *Publications* · Eugene, Oregon

MYSTIC TWINE
Musings of Mind and Spirit

Resource Publications
An Imprint of Wipf and Stock Publishers
199 W. 8th Ave., Suite 3
Eugene, OR 97401

www.wipfandstock.com

ISBN 13: 978-1-60899-254-6

Manufactured in the U.S.A.

To my parents
Both gone from the dream
But always in mind

Contents

Preface

Mᴜ ʟɪғᴇ ʜᴀs ʟᴇᴅ me down many paths and placed many masks upon my face. I have been a shy, timid boy, wary of the world and the people in it. I have been street-smart and profoundly foolish. I have allowed my need for cheap recognition to equip me with the fighter's fists, having boxed and later indulged in wild brawls in dance halls. I have been both very cool and a nerd when they weren't. I have tried to think, compete, work, and screw my way through life, hoping to find an answer or two in the process. I have been an athlete in many sports and enjoyed the exertion and fluidity of them all. I have loved (as much as my self-absorption would allow) and I have hated, albeit briefly and politely. I have been a father of three and a parent of six. I have survived three different serious accidents, wept from both sorrow and joy, succeeded and failed. I have battled and conquered rage, depression, mistrust, regret, and grief and have learned to live fairly with my brothers and sisters. My life has taken me down paths that dead-ended, hurt myself and dear others, and some that have even brought truth closer to my door. I have tried to run my own business and been a leader for others who have done a better job at running theirs. I stumbled onto a career as a software geek that allowed me to both hide from view and visibly contribute at the same time. I screwed up at that endeavor by being good enough at it to be promoted to management, which I was extremely ill-equipped to succeed at, even though I managed somehow to have a fairly satisfying and extended career. I have celebrated life at the arrival of my children and mourned the passing of a father, a mother, a dear uncle, and my only birth son.

In hindsight, it appears that all of these paths have led me to exactly where I needed to be; sitting here at my computer writing to a group of unknown readers of tales that I never even knew I could write. I have however always loved a good story, whether spun by a book, a movie, a poem, or a life. Now, in my own later life, I find that not only can I tell a decent story and have a few to tell but that I have always wanted to be just that, a storyteller. When I first started receiving and scribing poetry, I was somewhat flattered that, by whatever causal cosmic accident or appointment, I could now consider myself a poet. That was until I actually tried to get poetry publishers interested. As it turns out, my poems bear little resemblance to modern verse. Of this, I am grateful. My poetic interests gravitate more towards the musical odes of The Eagles, Bob Dylan, and Van Morrison, or the spiritual gems of Emerson and Rumi. Until a year ago, I had read very little poetry, understood even less of it, and wrote only casually. I found that the only non-musical rhyme I truly loved were the ones that told stories, like the *Ancient Mariner* or *Casey at the Bat*, or ones that inspired me spiritually and left hope as the reader's inheritance. I have also retained a special place in my heart for joyous humor and a healthy respect for the redemptive and therapeutic value of laughter. All of these things have, each in their own way, shaped me as poet and storyteller.

I find the material world to be an absurd place. After many years of fighting it, insisting it change, and detesting it, I now simply let go and accept it as such. In fact, I have learned to include it in my repertoire of humorous topics and find in it an almost endless reservoir for my writing. Truly scrutinizing the world we live in leaves us with but two choices; delude ourselves as to its efficacy and authenticity or look for a better actuality. Both are valid pursuits and both offer different rewards and pitfalls. I have pursued the former, found it lacking, and now practice the latter.

As you read this book, keep in mind the many life-tracks of the author that have shaped his writing and perception of the world. Bear in mind the aforementioned bias towards storytelling and the love and wonder of the spiritual mind and life. Know that my various adventures, my spirit, and the love of God have led me to a place I am unable to aptly describe or even fully assimilate. From my origins and the place where my destiny has deposited me, I invite you to enter into a pact of sorts. I ask you to open your mind, leave all preconceived notions of reality behind, and come with me on a journey. It is as new and valuable a journey to me as it will be for you. Together, I pray we may rediscover a place lost to us since the beginning of time and space; a place where we do no violence, neither accept nor defend meaningless baubles, or restrict our minds to the narrow constraints of science, popular notions, or fixed beliefs. Let us find a place offered by the Creator of all there is; where intelligence is unimaginable and unlimited, where joy abounds, and where love unifies in a way that transcends our differences. Let us entertain the possibility that all we take for granted may be false, that our beliefs may simply be an artifact of societal and parental repetition, and that a universe and nature as complex and as beautiful as ours must have an origin beyond our comprehension. And most of all; let us acknowledge that certainty, lasting peace, oneness, and eternal life are unavailable here. As the Buddha once said, "All that we are is the result of what we have thought." If he was right, could it be that our (errant) thoughts have collectively formed the world we take for granted as real? And if we have established a life separate from our Creator, is it not possible that our separated mind is responsible for those same thoughts? And is it not just as likely that the wholeness of the (un-separated) Divine Mind would produce a far superior reality, if only we had access to it?

All I request for admission to this mystical voyage is your willingness to temporarily suspend existing beliefs and admit other possibilities exist. We do it regularly when we attend movies, listen to lectures, or in conversation with friends. Do we not owe it to ourselves to consider the possibility of a more certain, more loving, and eternal existence as an alternative to the violent, unstable, and often treacherous world we daily abide in? As the man once said, "What do you have to lose?" So come with me, sisters and brothers (for we truly are, you know) and let us explore some alternatives. I promise it won't hurt and you just may find that you have enjoyed our little cerebral/spiritual adventure. So join me now as we reflect on the ball of mystical twine that is ours to unravel.

Mystic Twine

Mystic Twine 06/09
A new one started
Scheduled at the tone of time
A rare volume appointed
To infuse the rhyme
More on love and all good things
All staggered within the lines
Wonderful stories and tales
To uplift in modern times
Trip with me, sisters and brothers
Canyons run throughout the rhyme

Trackless Time

You don't buy poetry by the pound
In fact, you can't buy it at all
Tis but a tasty morsel to nibble on
A bit of gratis cerebral delight
Mind bubble burst, just for you
The fireworks, yours to behold
A fiery confrontation
Best left in prison hold
Savor each tidbit of rhyme
Keeping sync with trackless time

Let's Mingle

Black and white
Do or die
Two sides of an empty flap
Determined to tell us why
A choice must be made
To be good or bad
Arbitrary decisions
That must be had
Forced into belief in duality
Indicated by separate ways
Choose left or right, up or down
Just meet in the middle some day
An illusion of divisibility
A sutured mind to see
Whatever flossed our eyes over
Left me as blind as thee
See straight with one eye
The pairs merged into singles
The two into and from the One
All together now, let's mingle

Call Me J

A pen name, a matter of choice
Small dishonesty to taint the play
No matter, it's all just illusion
That we come to see someday

No secret identity intended
No mask to the masquerade
Simply a means of retraction
From lowly thoughts gone astray

I like the way it stacks the day
I'd really like to see me
In tune with what I pray

So if I hide beyond answer
And distil to you no better
Know that I'm 99% lighter
When facing you this way

A further quirk of understanding
Leaves me with little to say
Only that I much like the fact
That now you call me J

Close Proximity

My heart sings for you
Lost son
Golden haired boy
Heart of the sun
Gentle, simple, undemanded joy
Irrepressible singing spirit
You were my wandering boy

Death called at such a young time
Barely a man had begun
Innocent to me you were
Though not by the world's song

I finally saw you at last
Yet a moment too late was I
To know what would be lost
When you, sweet boy
Lived no more, at my cost

Yet alive you became
After crossing death's door
You come to me holy now
Close proximity forevermore

Business Fable

I will always be a fan, Charles Schwab
Of the excellence brought to bear
On workplace and work ignited
And for letting me employ there

The people were all quite fine
A lovely lady for boss
A well run enterprise for sure
The leaving was my loss

The sacrifice only an illusion
But I appreciate the thought
Impregnated by the time together
Look what you have wrought

I work now for a greater Master
Although you were quite able
Quite a joy to have been there
Thank you for the fable

Tidbit of Bliss

My life is not a snore
It is much, much more
It is more than a snore

A tiny eyeful to see
A mere cross section of the whole

Have we not judged and dismissed
Our brothers as guilty in this
This tidbit of knowledge
This tidbit amiss

As they say, ignorance is bliss

Be Different

Be fair, Mr. Obama
Be true and honest and brave
It will be quite the uphill battle
It will likely draw you down
Yet never let it defeat you
You have much to take account
Leaders less talented
Have come and gone
Taken us to the brink
But you, my friend
Will harken us back to Heaven
If only you will dare to be
Different

A Little Tradition

I'm not much for tradition
But I love people who do
I'll accept a little of the past
If it pleases only you

For you mean much more to me
Than some Tin Lizzie belief
We share love, you and I
We come from common relief

The same Father
Promulgated us all
Left us to come together
Shortly before the fall

So a little tradition
As you can see
Is quite okay by me

Hooters Dilemma

As I sit across from Hooters
Contemplating the irony
Of writing spiritual poetry
While looking at pictures of boobs

I am amazed at our dexterity
At our movement, to and fro
You gotta have a sense of humor
To be able to take it as so

The big and small of it
The roundness and fullness
That somehow fits

I guess I'll need to make
A decision about which way to go
Considering all of the features
Both, one helluva show
(Boobs are the last to go)

Texas Sky

Fastest clouds in the sky
Drifting on courageous face
Watching them fly by
I'm a little amazed at the pace
It's almost as if they're looking
For someone to start a race

Breezes departing now
I'm left here warm and sticky
But I'm still doing my stuff
Even when it feels icky

Common Think

I won't be going back to work
I see the future ahead
No more nine to five for me
Finally awakened from my dread

Armed now with pen and paper
I lay down my formulated plans
I'm likely a lot more suited
Than originally thought I can

It's obvious we missed something
I haven't yet run out of ink
Still cranking out the bullets
Of love and common think

Stateless

Leave the state of mind behind
Good or bad it be
Welcome to a clear Mind
Devoid of hate and greed

No such place as Iran
The myth of Korea as such
Both just unruly symbols
Showing us significant much

These states are not out there
Problems of someone else
The mystery of such illusions
Is they exist within ourselves

Pack up, move out
Relocate as soon as possible
I know a place of clarity
Where stateless we may be

Pray and Play

My wife and I
Love each other dearly
Yet there are those moments
When I tend to piss her off
But we get back in the saddle
Let differences fall where they may
I'm not trying to piss her off
No matter what they say
She means the world to me
I would rather die than betray
I really don't like pissing her off
I would rather we pray and play

The Exchange

I have seen wondrous things
Properties not deeded here
Things far more profitable
Than what we see as near

It takes a bit of awakening
And admitting we are asleep
But oh, my friends
The treasure that waits within

We have settled for so little
When all was what we had
Our Father offers everything
For the nothing we hold so dear

Keep looking, my lonely brother
His Hand extends until we find it
His Heart welcomes us Home at last
Quite worth the exchange well cast

Hummingbird Poop

I saw a hummingbird poop
Amidst all his lovely things
The fluttering, the flying
With those oh so tiny wings
Walking on air, wind at his knees
The little guy is a joy to behold
If just for the moment to please
I thanked him for the offer
To lend me his airy peace

Exquisite Direction

Such exquisite direction
I receive from Master so fair
Touching me ever so lightly
Requesting me to reaffirm
All direction previously asked for
And redeemed for so much more
Guiding my every nuance
Every step my feet must take
I have requested it as such
I love and cherish its touch
My soul smiles in delight
My mind so very at rest
I'm sliding Home on an ice wave
Safe, free to leave the past

The Nation We Tell

We've been to war with the English
The French confronted as well
Not to count the native Indians
The Spanish got in there, do tell
Other countries weren't enough
So we fought ourselves through hell
The Germans, next on our list
The Italians and Japanese
All in the mix as well
The Russians, the Vietnamese, the Koreans
The Iraqis, who so easily fell
Granting their oil for sale
I wonder who is next on our list
For the peace loving nation we tell

American Pie

We have the largest slice
Of the pie American made
Everyone else wants a piece
All for a bite to be had

We better get out our spatula
Stand ready to defy and defend
That big ole savory pie
Else all will be taken
Leaving us little to spend

What price, you say, for the defense
Well our souls, of course, my friends
Give the whole damn thing away
Stand richer at the end

Mighty Grand

I have never been contained
In this tiny little frame
Have been long since housed
In the limitless fame

Words will struggle here
I tread unreported ground
I'll give it my best shot though
We'll see if we can hold it down

Likely, it will be too light for us
Too airy to take in hand
You'll just need to take my word for it
It's looking mighty grand

Divinely Fair

A view of things quite different
A perspective seldom used
A bit out of the ordinary
Not nearly the normal ruse
Simple and open it remains
True since the beginning of all
Seldom reported or syndicated
No amusement value at all
We may not be ready to accept it
Our minds may be somewhat impaired
Still, we ought really to consider it
To be at divinely fair

I Am

I am holy
And well pleased
I am eternal
For a very long time
I am free
To be
I am whole
The finding of my soul
At peace forever
Where else would I be
In the Heart of God
Forever with Thee

1

---

1. All odd-numbered lines from *A Course in Miracles, Manual For Teachers*, page 38.

Release From Time

We come from our potential
All the rest is just playing the game
The finish was the start
Walking backwards since we came
The joy of the truth is
We remain at the finish line
Soul standing motionless
Awaiting release from time

Listen for the Love

The power of the verse
The form no matter
The content the same
The rhyme, the reason
Culled from golden frame
All complete divinations
Of love's pearly game
So listen for the love, my friend
Ignore the eyes and ears
It will come most assuredly
Evaporating the fears
Let nothing deter your drive
Let nothing dissuade your will
Listen for the love, my friend
Acutely, yet you must be still

The Whole of the Parts

We are but pieces of the Whole
Nothing special or different
Nothing to get excited about
Excepting the Sum of the parts

That grand total, my friends
Is a sum without a pair
A composite much too grand
To be dissected or compared

Accept what we are, dear brother
Assimilate the Whole
Forget about our differences
Bid love and join our souls

So much more to live for
So little to leave behind
Greater than any here bequeathed
The mind but a part of the Mind

The priceless given for the valueless
Heaven for hell, the trade
So much of a bargain offered
For wholeness, Heaven-made

The Joining of Our Souls

I have become what was promised
The soul golden gilded
Love being all around
Fulfilling all that was offered
All that I dreamed be true
A something never envisioned
A nothing to leave behind
Accepting the same gift tendered
To all of you as well
Nothing with only my name on it
Everything owned in whole
By the coming together of all of us
The joining of our souls

Moon Walker

It's the way you move, Michael
Your elegance in rapid beat
It's the way your soul expresses
And dances upon your feet

The body used as art form
With music and words as fare
Performing something quite different
No fellow artist to compare

I don't mind a little strangeness
I find it becoming in my friends
But what you brought, dear brother
Will haunt me until my end
Beguile me with its wonder
Leaving nothing to extend

In Your Wake

Big hearts make for big targets
So sorry Michael, for fear's assault
Blind eyes can see no love
They hear no hymns
And say no prayers
Angels walk among us
On fine and sunny days
So sad to see you go, Michael
You left so much love
In your wake, in your wake

Given Prize

My book of choice
The blue and gold
Divine treasure given
Left for me to hold
Every day a blessing
Every word a prayer
Filling my life with love
Amid thoughts so very fair
My Brother speaks to me thus
He blesses my very eyes
He comes to me naked
His truth, the given prize

Three Prayers

Dear Father
There can be no greater gift
Than to be Your Son
None

I know love now
My heart swells
Soon to burst
Filling the universe

Whatever You would have me do
I will do
Whatever You would have me say
I will say
Whatever is Your Will for me
I will pray

Short Blessings

Blessed Father
You have made me whole
Free and eternal
Safe forever
In the Heart of Your Soul

Thank You for the living
Dead no longer
Forever born
Alive again and breathing
The life thought forlorn

Divinely Spent

Those sweet, delicious moments
If only they would stay
The times no longer alone
The moments for which I pray

Composing my finest hour
The holy instants that come about
To bring me sweet joy and bliss
My Beloved calls them out

Holy thoughts on Heavenly breezes
Gifts from Paradise sent
Those sweet, delicious moments
Each divinely spent

No Words to Defend

I deal in words
Most every day
This way or that
I seem to find a way
To tell you all about it
This strange and wonderful thing
I hope my words will inform you
And ring the golden bell, ring
I do my best
I'll have you know
I give it my all
In hopes that I will show
That all you see before you
And all you hold so dear
Will someday need to leave you
Come out from behind the fear
And when that wondrous thing happens
I will do my best again
And when that brilliance steps forth
There will be no words to defend

The Storyteller

The one who weaves the tale
He or she who tells
Of wonderful, imaging scenes
That spin the magic spell

Knowing how all will end
Not part of the bargain made
Just telling what he's seeing
Upon the mind's blueprinted way

The years have added to wisdom
Some likely things unknown
Working them throughout the tapestry
The story breathes on its own

Characters and cast come to life
To strike the unlikely pose
Whilst the storyteller continues
To tell the tale, in poems and prose

Poems Delivered

I believe I delivered it faithfully
This very first book of poems
That now I hold in my hands
World born at last, it appears

I read them now with gifted love
As much treasure now as then
When first they came upon me
Delivered by way of my pen

The Poet's Quill, my child
Golden words entrusted to me
While in the process of gestation
I knew not what it would be

This tiny book of treasures
That emanated from my hand
I have done my job, sweet Brother
I have carried the song this far
Now held in hand so lovingly
Faithfully joined with who we are

The Shall

To arrive at justice
Or enforce the rigid rule
To impart truth and wisdom
Or insist on laws too cruel

Shall we not just be fair
In our dealings
Shall we not just get along
With each the other, our brother

Shall we not just honor one King
Who loves us without a bound
Who clearly and fully embraces
The shall that will surely be found

Imperfect

It seems I need to introduce
My imperfections for all to see
Speech or book, no matter
Apparently, this is my fee
For believing in material perfection
And agreeing to live its creed
Tis but a laughable belief
I need to give up the notion
That here we find relief
Perfection, it seems, grows only
In holy fields of divine seed
Who gives a damn about worldly things
When Perfection is all I need

A Bad Case of the P's

You are the perfect purveyor
For my potentially potent
And purposely pointed poems
We can both now probably partake
Of a portion of persistently patient
People in the form of particular populace
Petitioning our sense of perfection
Persuading us to peek, perhaps
At the point where peace prevails
Coming to print in poet's pages
Perchance a popular possibility
Pinning down all potentialities
Placing the pieces precisely apart
I really need to stop with the P's
It's provoking partial participation
And bringing me to my knees

Soul of Home

The body is temple not
A façade at best it can be
A distraction, in form, from truth
The ego's garb to see

The mind and heart is sanctuary
From all we would little be
A place of glorious fashion
For all the heavens to see

Value flesh not, for it has so little
As compares a flicker to flame
It is such a minute distraction
And bears no hope for fame

Use it only as vehicle
But make it not your own
Claim instead the gift from Heaven
The endless Soul of Home

Get It

Some will get this book
And some will not
Some will get it
When they get it
And some will not
Some won't get it at all
It won't even touch their mind
So I hope you get it
Get it?

Our Father's Flock

Think what you will
Think what you may
These words are truly delivered
In your heart, they are meant to stay

Let not perception trip you up
Allow no illusion to mask
The truth so finely given
Though it may take you to task

Your beliefs, it may surely challenge
Your foundation may surely rock
And if this be so, I pray
May it awake you to our Father's flock

Form of Reality

If the world be true
Then why must it falter
If it be real
Why must it fail
Nothing holds true within it
Little survives the test
For if the test of truth
Be what is real and enduring
How may the world then pass
When all it does and is
Fails and cannot last

Even death, it seems
Has shown exception to the rule
As sweet Jesus has shown us
A belief fit but for a fool
For if a thing is proven
To never be absolute
Do we believe what does not hold
Or that which proves it untrue

Love is all that holds and lasts
All else will fade away
Nothing in man's world survives
Nothing in truth will stay

Can life be truly composed
Of things that falter and die
Of decay fostered beings
Or are they merely lies

Challenge we should
And accept we should not
A life that offers so little
Disregarding the one we forgot
For beyond this nightmare dreamed
Lies Creation fully bloomed
A place that lasts forever
A place with plenty of room
For lost souls who leave the error
Made so long ago
A place so real
We will instantly see
That what we now think as true
Will no longer be known to be

This righteous place, my friends
We call Heaven
Promised since time began
The only form of reality
That has truly ever been

Orphans

We are all orphans
Who were never meant to be
Plenary fragments of the Whole
Spun in troubled memory
Quite unnatural, the act
Heartbreaking, the plea
To think of wholeness lost
Drops me to my knees
Damn good thing it's only illusion
That deprived me of my family

An Inch Closer #1

I know some soul contenders
Mostly, an unsuspecting lot
They likely don't know what's happening
Or of the plan they are part
Conscious awareness not necessary
In such wonderful matters of heart

We have arrived at once
We have come to open the gate
Brothers in spirit together
Arriving at our fate
Come join us, reluctant others
Don't falter, don't be late
We come together at yonder point
Much to anticipate

When joined by love, our bond
One very large step we take
An inch closer to reality
A step closer to the gate

Long Time Coming

It's so wonderful to be back
Back in my Father's Heart
Starting, with joy, to integrate
Into the Whole, of which I am part
It's so nice to have such company
It's so nice to hold you all
I've been a long time coming
I'll see you past the fall

Mystery Rhyme

There is both rhyme and non-rhyme
And some at different times
The words roll back and forth
To arrive at quizzical lines
A mystery formed to trick the brain
Yet fair Mind will foresee
All that lies within refrain
And all that is yet to be

Vain Attempt at Union

A vain attempt at union
The joining of bodies be
Often turned inside out
Turning love to attack, the fee

The banging of bodies
The clanging of form
Keeps changing the subject
Hoping to make sex the norm

Yet they keep on banging
Contained by ego's reclaim
Tis futile, this search for oneness
When attempted in flickering flame

No matter how close bodies perform
Union can never be
For oneness, my friends, may only be had
In Mind and Spirit of thee

A Higher Place

We find no pornography here
Only in small mind does it lay
The visible only a reflection
Of the ego mind's decay
A minefield of trouble
Laced with several delay
Many things to trip upon
To cause us much to repay
Worthless time spent in endless repair
A false residence with unpaid rent
We may choose this home of misery
We may hang here in life poorly spent
Or move we may, to higher ground
To a place where all will be sent
A larger Mind quite magnificent
A much more appealing fate
A grander place to live and place
Purest thoughts upon our plate

Paradise Lost

The mind is not stinky
The mind is not flat
Leading us forward
Towards beauty at last
Absorbed by the larger
Pulled from the past
This mind prior loaned
To illusion well cast
Though lost there we may seem
Our Father forgets us not
His Call is never ending
Love carried on purest of thought
He beckons us forward
To leave this tiny plot
Come back Home, my brother
To Paradise rethought

Yours to Set Free

I have a right
To write what I write
No matter of right or wrong
Simply a means of commission
Of what has been given in song
It comes, I accept, and write it
No question or critic am I
My faith codes it successful
It needs not my caustic eye
It comes as needed
This I deem true
Not mine to decide or choose
I simply deliver the package
It comes minus the terms
Of which I could construe
To provide you true affirms
Yet I will not
For I trust it
Just the way it be
Take it or leave it
Yours to set free

Laid Low

The world is too hard
And I am made of softer mettle
Too much to deal with
Too conflicted to settle
For a life less noble
Than what I should do
Too many high expectations
From brothers who live quite low
I can't please anyone, even myself
Father, show me which way to go

Ageless Youth

The fountain of youth
Offers a sip
From waters forever gold
A glimpse into infinity
A simple eye to see
All that quenches the primal thirst
All that promises to be
The ageless youth of eternity

Be Your Own Critic

I will tolerate no critic
I simply don't give a damn
No one may choose for another
It's quite a personal thing
The critic may make light or heavy
With praise or judgment alike
It simply bears no relevance
To what we each must do
The signal travels a varied range
Intended for just a few
We all travel Home by sundry routes
The one we divinely choose
So pay no heed, my brother
Examine and decide for yourself
If this tome be meant for you
Else put it back on the shelf
Not to discard forever
The time may come around
When you and the words agree
When your soul is divinely found

Giving It My Best

Nothing to prove
No one to impress
Provides me an expanded chest
Or could these be simply fallen breasts
Either way, they're enlarging my dress
I might do something
By way of redress
Yet not very likely
That I light up a vest
I'll just have to live with it
I'm giving it my best

At Our Father's Feet

We are brothers
On the same quest, you and I
Tasked with the same goal
Led by the same Force
Quite a worthy goal it is
To gather our brothers around
To pierce the illusion profane
We know each other
If only by name
And of our efforts offered
Yet we are family
Of the only clan there be
Our paths may run in parallel
We may never actually meet
Til one fine day in Heaven
When we sit together
At our Father's Feet

All That is True

Let the world crumble
Let it fall where it may
Our Father watches over
Those who truly pray
For truth to arrive
And peace to stay
And stay it will
And no longer hide
Behind the false curtain
That shields it from our eyes
Lose nothing, we will
When the walls come tumbling down
Only clear sight will prevail
Desires and wants and needs
Will vanish ever so quickly
To be replaced by all we require
Nothing left but Paradise
Nothing left untrue
Once more, we see with clarity
Each other, and all that is due

The President of Michigan

The new American wasteland
Deserted factories and malls
Left behind to crumble
On lives who took the fall
For greed reaped upon them
Fear of uncertainty too
We all took the bait
All got hooked on our due
While all the time we knew
We took much more than a few
Gobbled up more than our share
Leaving debris in Michigan, once fair

Travel Home

We've done this before, my friend
I would but this be the end
Though I love the phrase turned
I would be the eternal Friend
My words no longer impart
To lend to earth's ear alone
No body, no form, no frame
Just sweet Christ, my aim
Not ever to leave my brother
Alone we can never atone
As one we travel Home

Endless Feast

If you love, share it
It's the natural thing to do
And if you be so blessed
To partake of God's fine feast
Don't forget to pass the goodies
Our appetites to appease
The main course will likely be
Much more than corn and peas
And the price far less than free
Only a willingness to share is owed
To partake of the endless feast

Loveless Sleepy Flings

I lay tempted back to sleep
From this life I would awake
The temptation far too appealing
The path from light to take

Back to the trance, the doze
Back to the dormant pose

I will awake, I take no other course
No matter how appealing the bait
I know it leads me nowhere
Thousands of years too late

Heaven awaits me now
An eternity wide awake
Never again to sleep or dream
Of hate and separate things
Never again to rest my eyes
In loveless sleepy flings

Ad Man

Buying my eyes
So I will buy his prize
Asking for a piece of mind
Attention to the product spent
Shall we let the ad man say
What we invite in this day
Or say, speak to the hand
So little you offer, so little you pay
For my mind's valuable estate
Keep trying, my brother
Learn how to relate
Then come back and see me
We'll discuss our mutual fate

We Christ

No i in We
We see by not seeing
The forest for the trees
The eyes do not serve us well
Too many things recalled
That do not exist at all
The truth waits beyond the curtain
Love will never tell
For it needs our given consent
We must ring the golden bell
Only then shall illusion depart
To reveal the truth beyond
When we see, at last, one another
As Christ begotten, the consented Son

Oneness Hailed

I come to realize
What some have
And some have not
There is no difference
There is no various plot
There is no play for real
Separate bodies and things
Are slats along the rails
Traveling past stark illusion
To the truth of oneness hailed

Different Rhymes

Saying the truth
In different ways
By no means alters
The essence of the way
It exists as one
Forever to stay
No matter how several the times
We state it in differing rhymes

The Greatest Book Ever Written

The greatest book ever written
Will someday be known to all
The guide to illusion denied
Brother Jesus speaking in verse
Our first direct conversation
With the one who got there first
The one who became the Christ

His words are quite shocking
But then again, so was his life
He showed us much sublime
He showed us what it meant
To live without fear of death
Because it was a lie

So when you are ready, my brother
Open the book and read
He will answer all of your questions
And leave you with nothing to need

Villains in Our Head

The villains in our head
Come alive to see us
Awake or in our beds
Residing inside for evil's sake
Waiting to be used against us
Hoping our souls to take

The scourge of the west
The wicked of the east
Can't wait to unleash the cowards
Upon my brothers to feast

For if I can unleash them
Perhaps they will leave me alone
Unfortunate for my brothers
Who have their own at home

Each having our own set of demons
Purely errant thoughts they are
Too bad we all project them
Upon each other's hearts

Let us turn inside for battle
Conquer our own where they be
Never again to deny our brother
His destiny to be free

The only evil there is, you see
Is that which is born of need
To feed the voracious ego
With fear and guilt and greed

Know our brother is not evil
Know that we are all free
As soon as we evict the intruders
Cease attacking our brothers
Who are as innocent as we can be

Beauty is born of beholder's eye
Evil, much the same
Dissolve it where it lives
Leaving in dust the villainous game

Let Gender Depart

Beloved sister
Think not I forget your name
Yet know this about the writings
They are genderless I claim

The words clothed in convenience
No slight or error made
You too are my brother
Born of genderless Father
All the same, our trade

The body proclaims separation
I deny it to be real
All that we are, sweet sister
Has only divine appeal

It matters not which parts we own
Just more to keep us apart
Know that we are all just children
Of a Father whose only art
Is to keep us as one together
And simply let gender depart

Prosetic

Let me digress
But for a moment
Wax a new way
Let me be prosetic

The words seep beneath
The straight and narrow
They deny the straightened line
Used in ways most poetic
Minus any limits or fines

Let us say what must be said
In rhyme, or without, no matter
Lest it miss the holy mark
Piercing the dark, to light

Fling away all constraint
Listen to prose and song
Toss away limit, my friend
Absorb it as it goes along

Sail it to divine waters
Wing it on softened breeze
Ride it to the Gates of Heaven
The ultimate goal to appease

Journey

What a wonderful adventure
You take me on, Brother dear
A ride of wondrous repute
A journey quite startling
One I will never refute
Each day, a discovery
Of just how loving You are
As you take me ever so gently
(Sometimes kicking and screaming)
To a place ever so far
A location far too appealing
To ever be known by car
A trip of immense proportions
A diversion from planet and place
A map devoid of direction
Plain as the nose of my face
A destination already arrived at
The place we know as Home
A wonderful journey to return there
We travel as one, but never alone

It Will Have to Do

The truth strains
Against words and limits
Of what I know and can do
I know I transcribe it in part
It's all my yearning will do
I pray it is enough
I hope it is so
I stretch to let it be more
The total will be
All that I have earned
And all that I am now
I give what I can
It will need to do somehow

The Soldier

The soldier fights
Puts his life on the line
Ready to relinquish his breath
All for the party line

His intentions quite noble
His heart in the right place
His body and soul misused
By those abusive of his race
Power needs pawns
In this unholy of place
To gather about the spoils of war
No matter the cost or dread
All for its own consumption
No matter how many be dead

These young, courageous men
Fighting for what they believe
Too easily deceived by those
Who care not for their peace

Though they risk their life and limb
To appease the sorry wants of those
Willing to bury these boys
Willing to weep as show

Forgive them, Father
For the lives they so lightly discard
For naught but corporate interests
They break the hearts in two
Of those who love the valiant soldier
And those who live for You

I'm a Writin

I'm bona fide, Clyde
So silly it may seem
But I got myself a book or two
Sittin on my shelf esteemed

I wrote those puppies
Don't you know it's true
One day I got to writin
Amazin what came through

I was pretty much exhausted
I didn't know how to react
Guess I'll keep on a writin
Til the Big Guy takes me back

No Mistakes

So little that doesn't go far
Silly little jingles
Or tragedies on par
With sonnets and love songs
Flowing to hearts afar

I'm never quite sure
How they will end up
After putting pen to paper
My thoughts to interrupt

I only know I must pen them
It's the journey agreed to take
Following on behind them
No folly to mistake

A Giggle Away

So you think
Heaven is devoid of humor
Well think again, my friend
I get it on good advice
The joy that is within
So laugh aloud and jiggle
Watch fear just fade away
Never be ashamed to be tickled
Heaven is just a giggle away

I Will Remember

I will remember
The vision lost long ago
I will remember
The holy hymn that left my lips
I will recall
All divine commemoration
The memory of my Father
The sight of my Brother in light
The feel of the Heavenly Home
A place where all is set right
I will remember
So help me God

Olive Branch

The fallen olive branch
Laying upon the earth
The hope for peace alongside
The offering, residing in dirt

It is the most precious of gifts
That which allows love in
Retrieve the branch, my brother
Let it deny all sin

We are all the Children of God
Let our coming together begin
Gather the branch to extend
For only peace will save us
And calm all war to end

One Heart, One Soul, One Mind

The times are not as eloquent
Nor the man
Plainer speech and written word
For the fan
Harder, more direct, the point
Simple as we can

Something lost, something gained
We make the case somehow
Commune with words and sounds
The essence of the plan

Someday the words will die
The sounds by their side
Sharing mutual thought
The Holy Mind to abide

Knowing, and being, each other
One heart, one soul, one mind
Holding close to our brother
Now joined as one, in kind

Enough

Close enough to Christ
To be creative
Aware enough of God
To know I am His
Near enough to Heaven
To get my foot in the door
One enough with love
To be its fair partner
Fine enough to be
All my Father
Would have me be
Enough to be free

The Man in the Corner

The man in the corner
As mystery, he appears to be
The man in the corner
Within him, I cannot see
Dark and shaded he remains
Deep in the shadows is he
Keeping his sight at bay
The man in the corner
I will know some day

Small World

A small world we live in
Shrinking every day
Borders slipping into oblivion
Disappearing in a vague sort of way

Better lines of communication
The internet, the middle way
Revealing secrets once held close
Sweeping corners of dusty prose

Little left to hide away
Leaving so much to say
And say we do
And much we show
In text, voice, and video

Yet we say so little that is new
Lest we say it in love, it's true
Lots of extra syllables
Tons of acronyms too
Communication parsed to its essence
The One that connects the two

The Ways of Heaven

Of this world, I know
I've been here quite a lot
The ways of Heaven, less certain
I once knew, but I forgot

Finding my way back is fruitful
I gather the wayward around
All of us lost and broken
But none of us forever bound

The way Home will come, I'm certain
The truth, its silent child
All aligned and aboard, we are
Prepared to traverse the wild

Let our travels begin at once
From here to there, we pray
Finding our way together
The journey, for us, the way

The Heart

No slice of Heaven available
For it cannot be taken apart
It is of oneness indivisible
It is the Creator's Heart
So if truth is what you seek
And illusion to be left behind
Accept your course as one
And shortly you will find
That to carve out but a part
Is to deny yourself the Heart

The Quill

The pen, the physical component
The book, the intellectual piece
The quill awarded however
In mind and heart at peace
The license to write
The leave to poet
Life and purpose now forged
Mine only to go toward it

Learn to See

Finding my way back
Through the Sea of Free Will
Has made it a tad bit difficult
I pale and struggle still
It can never be otherwise
Else we never claim free
But find we will, our way
As soon as we learn to see

Path Preferred

My search for work will parallel
The worldly way, I'm sure
Seek, yet never find
Will be the motto secured

Yet while I seek, I find
That which was always found
The diamond of heart and mind
Seeds my common ground

The sight so clear, I need not see it
The calling astutely heard
Having waited so long with yearning
For the path most surely preferred

Spot of Still

I look at where I've been
I review the forgotten day
Blindly stumbling and falling
Til I choose the better way

Every moment I reside here
Each step along the way
I cherish that one decision
To find a better day

I have yet to regret it
Certain I never will
My feet have touched the love-lit sky
Reaching the spot of still

Judgment Day

As judgment lessens
I find there is less to say
So many words of condemnation
The loss of love, the pay
The silence deepens
As we approach the way
The sound of peace it is
As we embrace the judgment day

Sans Fame

In blessed solitude, I write
The public life, I disdain
I pray my heart remains uncorrupt
As I disperse to the crowded domain

I yearn for brotherly connection
But not to be lost to the world
I lean upon worldly wisdom
And Christ to keep me sane

I will bravely go where given
To do what must be done
I will go among the naysayer
Christ to keep me strong

The truth will find its way
It will pierce the illusion profane
Alone or consumed, I remain
Its friend and ally, sans fame

Lies and Doubt

Truth needs no defense
It speaks but for itself
No verification is needed
It touches the Holy Self
A place where truth is known
A time when recognition tones
Man's law, it obviates
Convention, it defies
When the bell of truth is rung
Lies and doubt must die

Port of Call

I stand confident
As I lay down my oar
My Brother beside me
My Captain at the fore

The ship so lithely slips
Into the oceans so fair
The water calm as peace
Soft breezes part the air

The sun and moon no longer compete
The light will show us all
Gliding into the sunrise welcome
Paradise, our port of call

Out of the Closet

Time to come out of the closet
Admit the shortfall we own
Open our hearts to each other
Never again to be alone

No need to preach
Simply open your mouth
Ask politely to speak
Of terms of surrender
Consent to open the gate
No hiding or reason to do so
Ours, the foretold fate

Damn sophistication
To hell with false dignity
We know we need each other
To be what we must be

So vacate the closet
Admit we are the same
Extend ourselves to each other
Our true identity we claim

An Inch Closer #2

Dearest Father
Every inch closer to You
Is a joy that overcomes
That fills my heart with love
Begs tears from my eyes

Each thought of being closer
Fills me beyond compare
The gift exceeds the sublime
I have no words this fair

Nothing I could say will convey
This joy that holds me now
All in the world is but shadow
Fading away somehow

Everything here is pointless
As Your Heart becomes mine
The illusion now dissolving
Truth but an inch behind

Love

Yes, I said love
How must I mean it
When it arises from so far above
The word is inadequate and faint
It could never describe love
It would ever but taint
The love as given
By poet or saint

The Body Christ

Love is the connecting tissue
That weaves the body divine
No flesh or bones hung here
This is a body beyond time
One that denies human sight
It is the body of Christ
Born of Heaven's light
Far beyond its pale counterpart
It touches all there is
Not confined by time or space
Nor pain or loss of life
It is our true form, my friend
The abode that carries us Home
The body our Father owns

Mind Clatter

The more we know
The less we know
Of things that truly matter
Our knowledge grows
Of worthless things
All consumed by matter
Clear yon troubled mind
Clean up useless patter
Invite yourself in, my friend
To the Mind without the clatter

Tiny Pills

Small colored pellets
Nicely wrapped in plastic vials
All with purpose to heal us
Having exited market trials

Each, a moment of forgetfulness
Of the fear of which they conceal
Never dare to look closer
Regardless of how you feel

Some to appease us, some to fade
Off the coveted list
Some to prevent or mitigate
That awful, dreaded risk

Let us stay fat, dumb, and happy
And pop those pills as we may
Let us take them a little faster
To keep pace with the ailment parade

Better Sight

The world is insufficient
To drum up the money
To pay the price
For the smallest of love or wisdom

The greatest of treasures
Lies beneath the line of sight
Our focus much too fixed
On avoiding the eternal light

But if you were to look
Slightly beyond your view
Manifold blessings await
Waiting to be part of you

Though your eyes may close forever
Your sight has just begun
Wonderful unimagined things
As joyful as the Son
Clarity never believed possible
A vision of enormous appeal
Seeing beyond the apple cart
To the seed, in the core, past the peel

Lonely Scribe

The scribe, lonely scribe
Taking the solitary trail
Words and pen, his baggage
Seeking the Holy Grail

A life born of silence
Covering a limitless terrain
Searching caverns of mind
Obfuscating the brain

He stays the lonely course
He bears the lightest of crosses
His is truth to bring
His is the relief thing

Some day we may put down
All words and phrases
Share our mind open-hearted
Speak without the sound
Let the silence bring us round

Til then, he speaks
Until his Father bids silence
The scribe then ceases
And is still

Available Angels

Enough angels are available
To give us what we need
Ours to issue the call
They wait but to heed

We cannot see them, of course
But trust we may, they abide
Waiting in the wings
Heavenly support to provide

We can't hear them either
They make but silent sound
Yet they speak most profoundly
The echo it makes, comes round

We will simply need to trust them
And the Creator who sent them out
Their hand extends before us
Willing to help us move about

There, but to show us
The possible, when God does run
The show behind the show
Where we star within the One

Heavenly Mind

I promote no agenda
I care not which way we go
The Lord is my shepherd
He will appoint me so

I desire but one thing
That we travel it all as one
Walking parallel or in line, we go
Lock stepped with the Son

So provide me no feedback
I care not for yesterday's words
My mouth waiting to be filled
With sounds of the heavens heard

Expel all worldly crap-stuff
Let it not enter your mind
Follow the true bell ringing
And your soul will genuinely find
The path of the One is many
All leading to Heavenly Mind

Greybeards Unite

Greybeards unite!
Gather up all you carry
Bring it in rhythm and reason
A custom blend of insight
Invites us to seldom tarry

All of us may participate
The sum of the parts exceeded
An explosion of wisdom within
A blooming of all that was seeded

Consider not your retirement
You have way too much to show
Fodder for emancipation
Fare paid for where we go

One head of grey hair
One mind of genuine gold
Stand up and be known, aged fellows
Let the wiser story be told

The Choice

The choice is simple
There are but two ways to go
One remains in darkness
The other, the light to show

One offers the following
Death, sin, guilt, and fear
The other is but made of love
With eternity and freedom near

One leads to conflict
The other, the road to peace
The darker the way, the road to death
The light makes all of that cease

The one is offered by ego
The other, by God and Christ
The one, a solitary and fearful life
The other, whole and free of strife

So choose your path, my brother
Decide what appeals you most
A life of fearful conflict
Or one with the Holy Host

Two Worlds

I struggle between two worlds
I am pulled to and fro
The world of things of matter
And the life my soul deems gold

The one I know is false
Yet it tempts me so
The other is certainly true
And reigns as my ultimate goal

Although it seems to matter
The battle is in mind alone
Dark thoughts and lonely ideas
Or light to pierce the veil

Christ Mind or lowly ego
These are my opposed locales
I need but a touch from my Father
To remind me of what is real
To know that one is illusion
The other, my true appeal

Thoughts Given Form

The only things we need defend
Are the thoughts that intrude within
The world, you see, is only that
We project from the temple of sin

What we see, and hear, and feel
Is that we decide to accept
The thought of mind given form
That which our soul rejects

Insane idea gave birth to separation
The one that ousted us from Heaven
The Home where oneness is sovereign
The Thought of Christ, its leaven

A Moment of Weakness

A moment of weakness
An instant of pain
As I leave my inner Heaven
To visit the world again
It leads me to the darkness
It drops me to my knees
I'll pick myself up and stand
And promptly take my leave

Ultimate Realist

I am the ultimate realist
I fade from shadows played
I've learned to ignore the obvious
Look past the solid and mundane

Addressing the portal to reality
Going through its tiny hole
Piercing the vagrant veil
Looking lovingly at The Whole

Preparing to expand unendingly
Getting ready to leave this plane
Leaving behind much of nothing
The universe, ours to explain

How Can I?

How can I not be safe
When I abide within The One
How can I not be free
When The One will travel me
How can I not remember
When the Mind is all I see
How may I not be at peace
When peace is all I be

Winds of Change

The winds don't change unexpectedly
With our Captain at the helm
For once, we find some certainty
For once, we face no change

Amazing to think, how sure we are
How delightful to remember it now
Never again to fear uncertainty
Never again to care how
The world continues to sustain itself
How it wanes and waves
It is but a fleeting thought
It affords us not to stay

Why walk the road uncertain
When alternative travel attends
Why continue to float on the temporal
When eternity never ends

Lucky

I have a fine wife
A child who lights my life
Some might call me lucky
But I don't believe in such

The result of my life, has and is
Mightn't be universally acceptable
But born of God, it is

The Giver of all is too big to be
A chancellor of luck with dignity
So much more, He gives away
I simply accept a larger own
Of Heaven bestowed this way

A Matter of Trust

I could not but trust You
Knowing who You are
Knowing what You do
No one ever deserved such trust
No one, til You, it's true
My most holy of companions
Dearest Brother and Captain, I serve
No reason forever, to doubt
No superfluous cause for concern
When His Holy Hand bestows
The trust divinely earned

One Foot Ahead of Another

I don't know when or where
I will be where I need to be
Placing one foot ahead of another
Soon enough I'll see

I keep heading in that direction
Keeping my heart aligned in Mind
Still hoping for resurrection
And the love I will surely find

My Father has promised
It's quite enough for me
Whatever, whenever, and wherever
He wants me, I will be

More to Share

Never let my doubt or wavering
Deter you in the least
They are but fledgling thoughts
That I most certainly will never keep
They are but light knockings
Upon the door of Holy Mind
They are but feeble offerings
Of the ego left behind
The treasure before us
So much more than we will find
By opening the door to the lesser
And entertaining its dismal fare
So close the door, bar its way
We have so much more to share

My Catholic Brothers

To my catholic and other brothers
I tender this care to you
Though we may travel different paths
And varied gates gone through
We are still but holy brothers
We are children of the only God
We pursue the same returning
The same dream forgiven
The same truth sought
So place your hand upon my heart
And know we are both the same
Born of Holy Father
Born of Heavenly fame

Complete Simplicity

I emphasize only that of God
I diminish what language would exalt
My verse left bare of punctuation
Using only the purest of thought
The words are of such minor comparison
To the thoughts of which they speak
I use only those given in love
Amid its complete simplicity

Size Doesn't Matter

Size doesn't matter
In any or all of things
Its value quite insignificant
No matter the volume it brings

Big or small, black or brown
These are such trivial things
They are only minor differences
That shadow what we bring

For our offerings to each other
Don't consist of silly things
The truest of gifts are given
Wrapped in the love we bring

Unto Caesar

I render unto Caesar
All that occupies this place
I render unto Caesar
All that would ease his pain

You may take my earthly possessions
You may even bar my face
Titles may be falsely issued
To possess my lonely place

But take from me, you never will
The truth and all it brings
So have a ball with all my stuff
And all those other silly things